P9-BJE-257

dinner

marie claire

dinner

jody vassallo

marie claire

introduction

Whether you're the one manning the stove or the one being cooked *for*, there's surely no more important question to be asked on a daily basis than "What's for dinner?" And, if you are the regular provider of this most vital of meals, the question can be a tricky one. We all get busy—too busy to cook. Sometimes the thought of facing the supermarket gets to be way too much and pantry supplies become depleted. And, let's be honest, even the most dedicated of domestic goddesses have days when those all-important culinary juices just don't flow. Every cook needs an injection of inspiration from time to time, and if you're looking to give your culinary repertoire a bit of a shake-up, or simply want a new idea or three, you've come to the right place. *Marie Claire Dinner* is the kind of book that bursts with recipes that are fresh, stylish, and totally doable, running the gamut of smart-casual and simple, through to wow-factor dinner-party numbers. Pasta and noodle dishes have become the modern-day cook's favorite fallback, and you'll love the selection here. Deliciously slurpy hokkien noodles (with Asian greens and glazed tofu, for example, or with five-spice Szechuan chicken), udon (in scrumptious yakisoba sauce), and rice noodles are all included, and the new twists on old pasta favorites (roasted chunky ratatouille cannelloni or spicy eggplant spaghetti, for instance) will keep all the Italophiles more than happy. Fish fans will just adore the likes of swordfish stacks with salsa verde, lemongrass fish with sticky chili sauce, and the heady, spicy kick of Moroccan seafood tagine. Meaty offerings are a thoughtful mix of the comforting (like chili beef with cheese quesadillas and satay chicken and mushroom pies) and the quietly sophisticated: Think veal with capers and white wine, or rosemary filet mignon with blue spread next time you need effortless main fare that's bound to impress. With *Marie Claire Dinner* you'll never end with a fizzle, either—desserts are kept spectacularly easy but all have that unmistakable *something* that sets them apart from the run of the mill. Chocolate cake with drunken muscatels, passion fruit custard pots, Irish coffee semifreddo with praline shards . . . mmmmm. Now you can have complete confidence of sweet success in the kitchen!

contents

quick ideas

pickled Japanese vegetables: try daikon, cucumber, and umeboshi plum

French baguette topped with sun-dried bell pepper and arugula leaves

olives and margaritas make ideal table companions

hunks of ciabatta or other crusty Italian bread dipped in rosemary-infused olive oil

deep-fried shavings of orange sweet potato

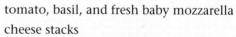

fresh oysters (and a squeeze of lime) served with champagne cocktails

puff pastry sprinkled with Parmesan and caraway seeds, rolled and baked

tomato, basil, and fresh baby mozzarella cheese stacks

quick ideas

baby zucchini with flowers fried in olive oil with slices of garlic

cherry and pear tomatoes mixed with cornichons, olives, and basil

warm peeled fava beans tossed with roasted garlic and shallots

mashed potatoes with extra-virgin olive oil, a pinch of saffron threads, and a dollop of mascarpone

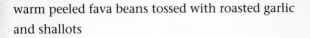

boiled peeled, halved baby beets, sprinkled with goat cheese and raspberries and drizzled with extra-virgin olive oil

blanched asparagus with toasted hazelnuts and a drizzle of balsamic vinegar

tomato, cucumber, and red onion drizzled with lemon juice and olive oil and sprinkled with parsley and sumac

tender wedges of roasted orange sweet potatoes drizzled with maple syrup and sprinkled with black sesame seeds

quick ideas

sheets of puff pastry cut into strips and sprinkled with coconut before baking

melted chocolate piped or drizzled into shapes on parchment paper and left to set

festive white and red currants or cherries set in small squares of flavored gelatin

try pear and brie crackers as a simple end to a meal

thick homemade custard laced with a good dash of your favorite liqueur

for chocoholics, try handmade chocolates with a chocolate milk shake

a spoonful of clotted cream with just about anything you can think of

chocolate-coated coffee beans served with hot chocolate

green tea sushi rolls

10½ oz dried green tea noodles
6 sheets roasted nori
½ cup pickled daikon, cut into long, thin strips
3 tablespoons drained pickled red ginger shreds
ponzu sauce, for dipping

Cook the noodles in a large saucepan of rapidly boiling water for 4–5 minutes, or until tender. Rinse under cold water and pat dry. Working on a flat surface, lay one sheet of nori onto a sushi mat. Top with one-sixth of the noodles along the bottom half of the nori, then arrange the daikon and the pickled ginger along the center of the noodles.

Roll the nori up firmly to enclose the filling. Cut the roll in half and then each half into three equal pieces. Repeat with the remaining ingredients. Serve with the ponzu sauce.

MAKES 36 PIECES

NOTE: Ponzu is a Japanese dipping sauce made from rice vinegar, soy, mirin, and dashi (fish stock).

noodles and pasta

yakisoba

1 garlic clove, minced
2 teaspoons grated fresh ginger
1/2 cup Japanese soy sauce
2 tablespoons rice vinegar
2 tablespoons sugar
1 tablespoon lemon juice
14 oz fresh yakisoba or udon noodles
1/4 lb pork tenderloin, thinly sliced
1 tablespoon sake
1 tablespoon sesame oil
2 cups shredded napa cabbage
3 scallions, sliced
1 carrot, thinly sliced
white pepper, to season
2 tablespoons pickled ginger

To make the sauce, place the garlic, ginger, soy sauce, rice vinegar, sugar, lemon juice, and 3 tablespoons of water in a saucepan and stir over low heat until the sugar dissolves. Bring to a boil and cook until the sauce thickens. Remove from the heat and allow to stand while you prepare the yakisoba or udon noodles by gently separating the strands.

Combine the pork and sake, and allow to marinate for 10 minutes.

Heat the oil in a wok, add the pork, and stir-fry over high heat until tender. Add the vegetables and cook until softened. Season with white pepper. Add the noodles and sauce to the contents of the wok and toss to combine and heat through. Serve the noodles topped with pickled ginger.

SERVES 4

noodles and pasta

barbecued pork ramen

5 cups chicken stock
1 garlic clove, halved
2 tablespoons Japanese soy sauce
1 lb Chinese barbecued pork (char siu), sliced
13 oz fresh ramen noodles
2 cups tightly packed baby spinach leaves
2 hard-boiled eggs, peeled and halved

Place the chicken stock, garlic, soy sauce, and one-fourth of the barbecued pork in a large saucepan and bring to a boil. Reduce the heat and simmer for 10 minutes. Strain into a large bowl. Discard the garlic and pork.

Cook the noodles in a large saucepan of rapidly boiling water for 5 minutes, or until tender. Rinse and drain.

Divide the noodles between four soup bowls. Arrange the remaining pork on top of the noodles, along with the spinach and egg. Carefully pour the boiling stock over the ramen. Allow the spinach to wilt slightly before serving.

SERVES 4

egg noodles with asian greens and glazed tofu

10 oz firm tofu

3 tablespoons kecap manis

1 tablespoon mushroom soy sauce

1 tablespoon vegetarian oyster sauce

1 teaspoon sesame oil

3 tablespoons peanut oil

2 garlic cloves, minced

1 tablespoon grated fresh ginger

1 onion, cut into wedges

1 bunch yau choy, roughly chopped

1 bunch baby bok choy, roughly chopped

1 lb fresh thick Asian egg noodles, separated

Cut the tofu into ½-inch-thick steaks, place into a shallow, nonmetallic dish, and pour the combined kecap manis, soy sauce, and oyster sauce over the tofu. Allow to marinate for 15 minutes, then drain and reserve the marinade.

Heat the sesame oil and 1 tablespoon of the peanut oil in a wok over medium heat, add the garlic, ginger, and onion, and stir-fry until the onion is soft. Remove. Add the green vegetables to the wok and stir-fry until they are just wilted. Remove. Add the separated noodles and the reserved marinade and stir-fry until heated through. Remove from the wok and divide between four plates.

Fry the tofu in the remaining peanut oil until it is browned on both sides. Serve the noodles topped with the tofu, green vegetables, and onion mixture.

SERVES 4

noodles and pasta

green tea noodles with scallops

14 oz dried green tea noodles
2 tablespoons vegetable oil
1 lb scallops, without the roe
1 tablespoon grated fresh ginger
1–2 small red chilies, seeded and thinly sliced
3 scallions, sliced
2 lemongrass stems, white part only, thinly sliced
2 teaspoons Thai red curry paste
1²⁄₃ cups coconut milk
1 tablespoon fish sauce
1 tablespoon grated light jaggery or light brown sugar
garlic chives with flowers, to garnish

Cook the noodles in a large saucepan of boiling water for 4–5 minutes, or until tender. Drain and keep warm.

Heat half the oil in a wok and cook the scallops in batches over high heat for 1–2 minutes on each side, or until the scallops are browned on both sides. Remove and keep warm.

Add to the wok the remaining oil, ginger, chilies, scallions, lemongrass, and curry paste, and cook over medium heat until fragrant. Add the coconut milk, fish sauce, and jaggery, and bring to a boil. Reduce the heat and simmer for 5 minutes to thicken the sauce. Return the scallops to the wok. Place the noodles on four serving plates and pour the sauce and scallops over them. Garnish with garlic chives.

SERVES 4

shrimp and spinach tempura udon

UDON BROTH
14 oz dried udon noodles
1 teaspoon dashi granules
¼ cup Japanese soy sauce
1 tablespoon sake
1 tablespoon sugar

TEMPURA
1 egg, lightly beaten
¾ cup ice water
1 cup tempura flour
1 tablespoon black sesame seeds
16 raw shrimp, peeled and deveined, tails left intact
oil, for deep-frying
12 baby spinach leaves, washed and dried

Cook the noodles in boiling water for 5 minutes, or until tender. Drain. Place the remaining broth ingredients and 4 cups of water in a saucepan and bring to a boil. Reduce the heat and simmer for 10 minutes.

Place the beaten egg, ice water, flour, and sesame seeds in a bowl and mix gently with chopsticks to form a lumpy batter.

Cut slits in the belly of each shrimp to keep them from curling during cooking. Heat the oil in a wok until hot, dip the shrimp into the batter in batches, and then cook for 2–3 minutes until crisp and lightly golden. Repeat with the spinach leaves. Drain on paper towels.

Place mounds of the noodles in bowls, ladle the broth over them, and top with the shrimp and spinach.

SERVES 4

noodles and pasta

egg noodles with five-spice szechuan chicken

2 tablespoons oil

1²/₃ lb boneless, skinless chicken breasts, sliced

2 garlic cloves, minced

1 onion, cut into thin wedges

1 tablespoon Szechuan peppercorns, toasted and crushed

1–2 teaspoons five-spice powder

19 asparagus spears, sliced

1 lb fresh thick Asian egg noodles, separated

2 tablespoons soy sauce

2 tablespoons oyster sauce

1 tablespoon honey

Heat the oil in a wok, add the chicken in batches, and stir-fry over high heat until golden and tender.

Return all the chicken to the wok, add the garlic, onion, peppercorns, and five-spice powder, and stir-fry over medium heat for 3 minutes, or until the onion is soft and the spices are fragrant. Add the asparagus spears and noodles, and stir-fry for 3 minutes. Stir in the sauces and honey, and bring to a boil. Toss well and serve.

SERVES 4

noodle nests with char siu and gai larn

1/2 lb fresh flat egg noodles
2 tablespoons peanut oil
1 garlic clove, chopped
1 tablespoon grated fresh ginger
1 onion, sliced
1 lb Chinese kale (gai larn), cut into 2-inch pieces
1 lb Chinese barbecued pork (char siu), sliced
1 tablespoon kecap manis
1 tablespoon oyster sauce
1 tablespoon soy sauce
2 tablespoons sesame seeds, toasted, to garnish

Cook the noodles in boiling water for 2 minutes. Drain well and keep warm.

Heat the oil in a wok, add the garlic, ginger, and onion, and stir-fry until the onion is soft. Add the Chinese kale and stir-fry until it is bright green and tender. Remove and divide between four plates.

Add the pork to the wok with the combined sauces and stir-fry until heated through. Spoon the pork over the greens, leaving the sauce in the wok. Form the noodles into nests and place on top of the pork. To serve, drizzle with the extra sauce from the wok and sprinkle with sesame seeds.

SERVES 4

stir-fried rice noodles with black bean fish

3 tablespoons peanut oil

1 lb swordfish, cut into bite-size pieces

2 garlic cloves, minced

1 tablespoon grated fresh ginger

6 scallions, cut into 1¼-inch lengths

2¼ lb fresh rice noodle sheets, sliced into ½-inch strips
   or 2¼ lb medium rice ribbon noodles

½ cup canned black beans, rinsed and drained

2 tablespoons bottled black bean sauce

2 tablespoons Chinese rice wine

1 tablespoon rice vinegar

1 tablespoon soy sauce

2 tablespoons sugar

½ teaspoon sesame oil

1 tablespoon garlic chives, cut into 2-inch lengths

Heat 2 tablespoons of the peanut oil in a wok, add the swordfish in batches, and stir-fry over high heat for 3 minutes, or until golden. Remove and set aside. Add the remaining peanut oil to the wok and stir-fry the garlic, ginger, and scallions for 2 minutes, or until fragrant. Add the noodles and stir-fry until soft.

Add the black beans, bean sauce, rice wine, vinegar, soy sauce, sugar, and sesame oil, and stir-fry until the sauce boils and thickens slightly. Return the fish to the wok along with the garlic chives. Toss to combine and serve immediately.

SERVES 4

preserved lemon chicken with fettucine

2 tablespoons oil
1 tablespoon ground cumin
1 tablespoon ground coriander
1/2 teaspoon cayenne pepper
1 onion, sliced
3 garlic cloves, sliced
1/2 preserved lemon, cut into fine shreds
1 lb boneless, skinless chicken thighs, cut into thin strips
1/2 cup lemon juice
1 cup plus 3 tablespoons chicken stock
1 cup green olives stuffed with sun-dried tomatoes, sliced
4 tablespoons butter
1/2 cup cilantro leaves
1 lb fettucine

Heat the oil in a large, deep frying pan and cook the spices, onion, and garlic over medium heat for 5 minutes, or until the onion is soft and the spices are fragrant.

Add the preserved lemon and chicken, and cook over high heat until the chicken is browned. Add the lemon juice, stock, olives, and butter, and bring to a boil, then reduce the heat and simmer for 10 minutes. Remove from the heat and fold in the cilantro.

Meanwhile, cook the pasta in a large pan of boiling water until al dente, then drain. Toss the pasta through the sauce and serve immediately.

SERVES 4

NOTE: Preserved lemons are available from delicatessens, specialty food stores, and Middle Eastern groceries.

noodles and pasta

squash with creamy bacon pasta

¼ lb fettucine
1 tablespoon oil
1 leek, white part only, sliced
3 slices bacon, chopped
½ cup dry white wine
1 cup light whipping cream
½ cup grated Parmesan cheese
4 large golden nugget squash

Preheat the oven to 350°F. Cook the pasta in a large saucepan of rapidly boiling water until al dente, then drain. Cut into shorter pieces.

Meanwhile, heat the oil in a frying pan and cook the leek and bacon over medium heat for 5 minutes. Add the wine, stir well, and bring to a boil. Stir in the cream and Parmesan, and boil for 3 minutes, or until thickened slightly. Add the pasta and toss together.

Slice the tops off the squash and use a spoon to remove the seeds. Fill the squash with the pasta mixture, then place on a baking sheet with the squash tops. Bake for 40–50 minutes, or until the squash are tender. Replace the tops to serve.

SERVES 4

ruote with gorgonzola and peppered steak

1 lb ruote (bite-size pasta wheels)
1 lb sirloin steak
cracked black pepper, to coat
1 tablespoon oil
1 bunch arugula
1²/₃ cups gorgonzola cheese, crumbled
1½ cups bottled pimientos, drained and sliced

DRESSING
¹/₃ cup plus 2 tablespoons red wine vinegar
2 tablespoons honey
2 tablespoons red currant jelly
2½ tablespoons extra-virgin olive oil
1 tablespoon whole-grain mustard

Cook the pasta in a large saucepan of rapidly boiling water until al dente, then drain.

Coat the sirloin steak in cracked black pepper. Heat the oil in a frying pan and cook the beef until medium-rare. Allow to rest for 5 minutes before slicing.

Add the steak, arugula, gorgonzola, and pimientos to the pasta and toss together.

To make the dressing, place the red wine vinegar, honey, red currant jelly, oil, and mustard in a small saucepan and bring to a boil. Boil for 5 minutes, or until thickened slightly. Pour over the pasta and toss well. Serve immediately.

SERVES 6

noodles and pasta

rigatoni with chorizo, chipotle chilies, and deep-fried basil

1 tablespoon oil
1 red onion, sliced
4 chorizo sausages, cut into thick slices at an angle
1²/₃ cups canned chopped tomatoes
2 canned chipotle chilies, chopped
oil, for frying
20 basil leaves
5½ cups rigatoni

Heat the oil in a large frying pan and cook the onion over medium heat for 3 minutes, or until soft. Add the sausages and cook for 5 minutes, draining off any excess oil. Add the tomatoes and chipotle chilies, and bring to a boil. Reduce the heat and simmer for 15 minutes, or until the sauce has thickened slightly.

Heat 1½ inches of oil in a deep frying pan over medium heat and fry the basil in batches until crisp. Drain on paper towels.

Meanwhile, cook the pasta in a large saucepan of rapidly boiling water until al dente, then drain.

Serve the sauce over the pasta and garnish with the fried basil.

SERVES 4

lamb pasta stroganoff

1 lb fresh herb spaghetti
2 tablespoons oil
1 lb lamb tenderloin
3 tablespoons butter
1 onion, sliced
2½ cups button mushrooms, sliced
2 tablespoons tomato paste
1 tablespoon whole-grain mustard
1⅓ cups sour cream
1 tablespoon thyme

Cook the pasta in a large saucepan of rapidly boiling water until al dente, then drain.

Heat the oil in a large frying pan and cook the lamb over high heat until browned and medium-rare. Leave to stand for 5 minutes before slicing thinly.

Melt the butter in the pan and cook the onion over medium heat for 3 minutes, or until golden. Add the mushrooms and cook until browned. Remove the onion and mushrooms and set aside.

Return the lamb to the pan and add the tomato paste and mustard. Reduce the heat, add the sour cream, and cook until heated through (do not allow to boil, or the sour cream will split).

Toss the sauce through the pasta. Serve topped with the onion and mushrooms and sprinkled with thyme.

SERVES 4

saffron fettucine with garlic seafood

3/4 lb fresh saffron fettuccine

1 tablespoon extra-virgin olive oil

1/2 lb scallops

1 lb raw shrimp, peeled and deveined, tails left intact

1/2 lb firm whitefish fillets, cut into large pieces

1/2 cup dry white wine

1/3 cup butter

3 garlic cloves, minced

4 scallions, sliced

thinly sliced zest of 1 lime

1 tablespoon snipped chives

Cook the pasta in a large saucepan of rapidly boiling water until al dente, then drain.

Heat the oil in a frying pan and cook the seafood in batches until the scallops and fish turn white and the shrimp pink. Remove from the pan and keep warm.

Add the wine to the pan and bring to a boil, stirring well to mix in any bits that are stuck to the bottom of the pan.

Add the butter, garlic, and scallions, and cook over medium heat until soft. Return the seafood to the pan to gently reheat and add the zest and chives. Twist the pasta into nests and serve topped with the seafood.

SERVES 4

ziti with brandy boscaiola

1 lb long ziti
1/3 cup butter
6 slices bacon, sliced
6 shallots, sliced
2 tablespoons brandy
8 1/2 cups mixed wild mushrooms
2 teaspoons thyme
1 cup chicken stock
1 cup light whipping cream

Cook the pasta in a large saucepan of rapidly boiling water until al dente, then drain.

Melt half the butter in a large frying pan and cook the bacon and shallots over high heat until crisp and browned. Stir in the brandy and bring to a boil, stirring to incorporate any bits stuck to the bottom of the pan.

Add the remaining butter to the pan, add the mushrooms, and cook to soften. Stir in the thyme, stock, and cream, and bring to a boil. Reduce the heat and simmer for 5 minutes, or until the sauce has thickened slightly. Serve on top of or tossed through the pasta.

SERVES 4

noodles and pasta

roasted chunky ratatouille cannelloni

1 eggplant
2 zucchini
1 large red bell pepper
1 large green bell pepper
3–4 ripe plum tomatoes
12 unpeeled garlic cloves
3 tablespoons olive oil
1¼ cups tomato puree
¾ lb cannelloni tubes
3 tablespoons shredded basil
½ cup ricotta cheese
¾ cup feta cheese
1 egg, lightly beaten
salt and pepper, to taste
½ cup grated pecorino pepato cheese

Preheat the oven to 400°F. Cut the eggplant, zucchini, bell peppers, and tomatoes into ¾-inch cubes and place in a baking dish with the garlic. Drizzle with the olive oil, and toss to coat. Bake for 1½ hours, or until the vegetables are tender and the tomatoes slightly mushy. Peel the garlic and lightly mash.

Pour the tomato puree over the base of a large ovenproof dish. Spoon the ratatouille into the cannelloni tubes and arrange in the dish.

Combine the basil, ricotta, feta, and egg, season well with salt and pepper, and spoon over the cannelloni. Sprinkle with the pecorino and bake for 30 minutes, or until the cannelloni is soft.

SERVES 6–8

noodles and pasta

46

fusilli with roasted tomatoes, tapenade, and mozzarella

5⅓ cups cherry or pear tomatoes (or a mixture of both),
  halved if they are large
5½ cups fusilli (spirals)
2 cups fresh baby mozzarella cheese, sliced
1 tablespoon thyme

TAPENADE
1½ tablespoons capers, rinsed and squeezed dry
1½ oz drained anchovy fillets
2½ oz canned tuna in oil, drained
2 small garlic cloves
1½ cups sliced black olives
3 tablespoons lemon juice
4–5 tablespoons extra-virgin olive oil

Preheat the oven to 400°F. Place the tomatoes on a baking sheet, sprinkle with salt and pepper, and bake for 10 minutes, or until slightly dried.

To make the tapenade, place the capers, anchovies, tuna, garlic, olives, and lemon juice in a food processor and mix together. With the motor running, gradually add the oil until the mixture forms a smooth paste.

Cook the pasta in a large saucepan of rapidly boiling water until al dente, then drain. Toss the tapenade and mozzarella through the hot pasta. Top with the roasted tomatoes and thyme, and serve immediately.

SERVES 4–6

noodles and pasta

chili linguine with chermoula chicken

1¼ lb boneless, skinless chicken breasts
1 lb chili linguine

CHERMOULA
2 cups cilantro leaves, chopped
2 cups Italian parsley, chopped
4 garlic cloves, minced
2 teaspoons ground cumin
2 teaspoons ground paprika
½ cup lemon juice
2 teaspoons grated lemon zest
⅓ cup olive oil

Cook the chicken breasts in a nonstick frying pan until tender. Leave for 5 minutes before cutting into thin slices.

Cook the pasta in a large saucepan of rapidly boiling water until al dente, then drain.

Meanwhile, combine the chermoula ingredients in a glass bowl and add the sliced chicken. Leave to stand until the pasta has finished cooking. Serve the pasta topped with the chermoula chicken.

SERVES 4

lasagna

1 tablespoon olive oil
2 garlic cloves, minced
1 large onion, chopped
1/4 cup pancetta, chopped
1 large carrot, grated
1 celery stalk, chopped
1 1/3 cups mushrooms, chopped
2 1/4 lb ground beef
3 cups canned chopped tomatoes
1 cup red wine
1 cup beef stock
1 teaspoon dried oregano
1 bay leaf
3 tablespoons tomato paste

1 lb spinach
1/2 lb fresh lasagna sheets
2 cups fontina cheese, thinly sliced
1 cup grated Parmesan cheese

CHEESE SAUCE
1/4 cup butter
4 tablespoons all-purpose flour
2 cups milk
3/4 cup plus 2 tablespoons
    ricotta cheese
1/2 teaspoon freshly grated
    nutmeg
1/2 cup grated Parmesan cheese

Heat the oil in a large frying pan and cook the garlic, onion, pancetta, carrot, celery, and mushrooms for 5 minutes, stirring. Increase the heat, add the beef, and brown well, breaking up any lumps. Add the tomatoes, wine, stock, oregano, bay leaf, and tomato paste. Bring to a boil, stirring, then simmer for 50 minutes. Steam the spinach to wilt; squeeze dry.

To make the cheese sauce, melt the butter in a heavy-based saucepan and add the flour to cook for 1 minute, making a smooth paste. Remove from the heat and slowly stir in the milk until smooth. Return to the heat and stir until the sauce boils and thickens. Cook over low heat for a minute, then stir in the ricotta, nutmeg, and Parmesan, and cook until melted. Preheat the oven to 350°F. Grease a 15-cup ovenproof dish. Layer one-third of the meat sauce, then lasagna sheets, then 3/4 cup of cheese sauce. Top with half the spinach and half the fontina. Continue layering and top with the Parmesan. Bake for 45 minutes.

SERVES 6–8

spicy eggplant spaghetti

2/3 lb spaghetti
1/2 cup extra-virgin olive oil
2 red chilies, thinly sliced
1 onion, finely chopped
3 garlic cloves, minced
4 slices bacon, chopped
1 large eggplant, diced
2 tablespoons balsamic vinegar
2 medium beefsteak tomatoes, chopped
3 tablespoons shredded basil
1/2 cup grated pecorino pepato cheese

Cook the pasta in a large saucepan of rapidly boiling water until al dente, then drain.

Heat 1 tablespoon of the oil in a large, deep frying pan and cook the chilies, onion, garlic, and bacon over medium heat for 5 minutes, or until the onion is golden and the bacon browned. Remove from the pan and set aside.

Add half the remaining oil to the pan and cook half the eggplant over high heat, tossing to brown on all sides. Remove and repeat with the remaining oil and eggplant. Return the bacon mixture and all the eggplant to the pan, add the vinegar, tomatoes, and 2 tablespoons basil, and cook until heated through. Season well.

Serve the spaghetti topped with the eggplant and sprinkled with the grated cheese and remaining basil.

SERVES 4 AS A STARTER

orechiette with peas and spinach

5½ cups orechiette
1 teaspoon olive oil
2 garlic cloves, minced
1⅓ cups ricotta cheese
1 cup chicken stock
1 cup peas (fresh or frozen)
3 cups baby spinach, roughly chopped
2 tablespoons finely shredded basil leaves
lemon wedges, to serve

Cook the pasta in a large saucepan of rapidly boiling water until al dente, then drain and keep warm.

Heat the oil in a large frying pan and cook the garlic over medium heat until golden. Add the ricotta, stock, and peas, and cook, stirring, until smooth. Simmer until the peas are tender.

Add the pasta, spinach, and basil to the pan and toss to coat. Cook just until the spinach leaves wilt. Serve with the lemon wedges and some crusty bread.

SERVES 4

warm casarecci salad

2 medium orange sweet potatoes
2 tablespoons extra-virgin olive oil
sea salt and cracked black pepper, to season
5½ cups casarecci
2 cups marinated feta in oil
3 tablespoons balsamic vinegar
19 asparagus spears, cut into short lengths
2¼ cups baby arugula or baby spinach leaves
2 vine-ripened tomatoes, chopped
3 tablespoons pine nuts, toasted

Preheat the oven to 400°F. Peel the sweet potato and cut into large pieces. Place in a baking dish, drizzle with the olive oil, and season generously with sea salt and cracked black pepper. Bake for 20 minutes, or until the sweet potato is tender.

Cook the pasta in a large saucepan of rapidly boiling water until al dente, then drain.

Drain the oil from the feta and whisk three tablespoons of the oil with the balsamic vinegar to make a dressing. Steam or microwave the asparagus until bright green or tender. Drain well. Combine the pasta, sweet potato, asparagus, arugula, feta, tomatoes, and pine nuts in a bowl. Add the dressing and toss gently. Season with black pepper and serve immediately.

SERVES 4

chu chee shrimp and scallops

CHU CHEE PASTE

10 large dried red chilies

1 teaspoon coriander seeds

1 tablespoon white peppercorns

1 tablespoon shrimp paste

10 Kaffir lime leaves, finely shredded

2 teaspoons grated Kaffir lime zest

1 tablespoon chopped cilantro stalk and root

1 lemongrass stem, white part only, finely chopped

3 tablespoons chopped fresh galangal

1 tablespoon chopped krachai (optional)

6 garlic cloves, chopped

10 red Asian shallots, chopped

18 fl oz coconut milk (do not shake the can)

1 lb raw jumbo shrimp, peeled and deveined

1 lb scallops

2–3 tablespoons fish sauce

3 tablespoons grated jaggery or soft brown sugar

8 Kaffir lime leaves, finely shredded

½ cup Thai basil

Preheat the oven to 350°F. Soak the chilies in hot water for 10 minutes. Drain, remove the seeds, and roughly chop. Place the coriander seeds, peppercorns, and shrimp paste onto a foil-lined sheet and bake for 5 minutes, or until fragrant. Place these ingredients, plus the Kaffir lime leaves and zest, the chopped herbs, garlic, and shallots into a food processor and process until a smooth paste forms. Add a little water if the paste is too stiff.

Spoon 1 cup of the thick coconut milk from the top of the can into a wok and heat until just boiling. Stir in 5 tablespoons of the chu chee paste, reduce the heat, and simmer for 10 minutes or until the oil begins to separate. Stir in the remaining coconut milk, shrimp, and scallops, and cook for 5 minutes. Add the fish sauce, jaggery, and Kaffir lime leaves, and cook for 3 minutes. Stir half the basil through the dish and garnish with the remaining leaves.

SERVES 4

seafood

oysters three ways

BLOODY MARY SHOT

6 oysters
3 tablespoons vodka
1/2 cup tomato juice
1 celery stalk, cut into small sticks
dash Tabasco sauce
dash Worcestershire sauce
salt and pepper, to taste

Place six oysters in six shot glasses, divide the vodka between the glasses, top with tomato juice, place a stick of celery into each one, and season with Tabasco, Worcestershire, and salt and pepper.

MAKES 6

CUCUMBER, GINGER, AND SESAME

3 tablespoons Japanese soy sauce
1 teaspoon sesame oil
1 tablespoon mirin
1 teaspoon sugar
1 cucumber
12 oysters in half shells
2 tablespoons pickled ginger
2 tablespoons sesame seeds, toasted

Place the soy sauce, sesame oil, mirin, and sugar in a small saucepan and heat until the sugar dissolves. Cut the cucumber into fine ribbons and place in the bottom of the shells. Top with an oyster, drizzle with the sauce, and sprinkle with ginger and sesame seeds. MAKES 12

PROSCIUTTO AND BALSAMIC VINEGAR SALSA

4 slices prosciutto
1 plum tomato, finely diced
1/2 red bell pepper, diced
1/2 yellow bell pepper, diced
1 small red onion, finely chopped
1 tablespoon chopped cilantro leaves
2 tablespoons balsamic vinegar
12 oysters in half shells
2 tablespoons crème fraîche or sour cream

Broil the prosciutto until crispy and allow to cool slightly before breaking into bite-size shards. To make the salsa, combine the tomato, bell peppers, onion, cilantro leaves, and balsamic vinegar in a bowl. Serve some salsa and prosciutto shards on each oyster, then top with a dollop of crème fraîche. MAKES 12

seafood risotto

2/3 lb mussels

3/4 cup plus 2 tablespoons dry
white wine

3 cups fish stock

pinch saffron threads

2 tablespoons olive oil

5 1/2 tablespoons butter

1 onion, finely chopped

1 leek, white part only, sliced

2 teaspoons grated lime zest

1 1/4 cups risotto rice

2/3 lb scallop meat

1 lb raw shrimp, peeled and
deveined

1/2 lb baby squid, cleaned and
cut into rings

3 garlic cloves, finely chopped

1 tablespoon chopped dill

Scrub the mussels and remove any that have opened. Place them in a saucepan with the white wine. Cover and cook over medium heat for 5 minutes, or until the mussels open. Remove the meat from the shells and set aside. Discard any unopened mussels. Add the fish stock and saffron to the cooking liquid; slowly bring to a simmer.

Heat the oil and 2 tablespoons of the butter in a saucepan, add the onion, leek, and lime zest, and cook over medium heat for 5 minutes or until golden. Add the rice and stir for 1 minute, or until translucent. Gradually add the stock to the rice, a cup at a time, stirring constantly until all the liquid has been absorbed and the risotto is creamy. Stir in half the mussels, scallops, shrimp, and squid, and cook for 5 minutes, or until tender.

Heat the remaining butter in a frying pan, add the garlic and the remaining seafood in batches, and cook over high heat until golden brown. Stir the dill through the risotto. Place the risotto in bowls and top with the fried seafood.

SERVES 4

herb-crusted tuna steaks with lentils and feta

1½ tablespoons butter

3 tablespoons extra-virgin olive oil

1 teaspoon grated lime zest

2 garlic cloves, minced

3 tablespoons chopped mixed herbs (sage, oregano, basil, parsley)

4 tuna steaks, trimmed of any blood

8 small vine-ripened tomatoes

⅔ cup marinated feta cheese

salt and pepper, to taste

1 cup French green lentils

1 bay leaf

1 tablespoon lemon juice

Preheat the oven to 425°F. Heat the butter, 2 tablespoons of the oil, the lime zest, and the garlic in a saucepan until the butter is melted. Add the herbs and remove from the heat. Place the tuna steaks on a shallow, nonstick baking sheet and pour the butter mixture over them.

Cut a small, deep cross in the top of each tomato, open out gently, and stuff with feta. Place the tomatoes on a separate sheet from the fish and sprinkle both sheets with salt and pepper. Bake the tomatoes for 20 minutes, or until soft, and bake the fish for 10–15 minutes, or until tender.

Boil the lentils and bay leaf together in a saucepan with enough water to cover them. When tender, drain and toss the lemon juice through with the remaining olive oil and any pan juices from the tuna. Serve the lentils topped with tuna and tomato.

SERVES 4

beer-battered fish with chunky fries

1 cup all-purpose flour
sea salt and pepper, to season
1 cup chilled beer
oil, for deep-frying
6 medium all-purpose potatoes, peeled and cut into thick wedges
4 large fish fillets or 8 small fish fillets

TARTAR SAUCE
¾ cup mayonnaise
3 tablespoons sour cream
6 dill pickles, chopped
2 tablespoons capers, rinsed and squeezed dry
2 tablespoons chopped parsley

Sift the flour into a bowl and season generously with salt and pepper. Whisk in the beer to form a smooth batter.

Heat the oil in a deep saucepan to 350°F, or until a cube of bread browns in 15 seconds when added to the oil. Cook the potatoes in batches until they are lightly golden. Drain on crumpled paper towels. Return the potatoes to the oil and cook until they are crisp and golden. Sprinkle with sea salt and keep warm.

Pat the fish fillets dry with paper towels. Coat the fish in the prepared batter and cook in batches in the hot oil for 3–5 minutes, depending on the size and thickness of the fish.

To make the tartar sauce, place all the tartar ingredients in a bowl and mix to combine. Serve with the fish.

SERVES 4

black bean crab

4 large blue crabs
1/4 cup peanut oil
4 garlic cloves, chopped
2 tablespoons grated fresh ginger
2 onions, finely chopped
3/4 cup canned salted black beans, rinsed and drained
1/4 cup fish stock
2 tablespoons oyster sauce
2 teaspoons fish sauce
2 tablespoons soy sauce
3 tablespoons black bean sauce
1 tablespoon superfine sugar

Clean the crabs and use a cleaver to cut each one in half or quarters (depending on the size of the crabs).

Heat the oil in a wok until smoking, then cook the crabs in batches until bright orange and tender, adding more oil with each batch if needed. Remove the crab from the wok and drain the wok of all but 2 tablespoons of oil.

Add the garlic, ginger, and onions to the wok and cook over medium heat until golden. Stir in the black beans, fish stock, oyster sauce, fish sauce, soy sauce, black bean sauce, and sugar, and bring to a boil. Return the crab to the wok and simmer for 5–10 minutes, or until heated through.

SERVES 4

swordfish stacks with salsa verde

SALSA VERDE

2 large handfuls Italian parsley, finely chopped

1 tablespoon dill pickles, finely chopped

2 tablespoons baby capers, rinsed and squeezed dry

1 tablespoon chopped anchovy fillets

4 garlic cloves, minced

3 tablespoons red wine vinegar

⅓ cup extra-virgin olive oil

1 large eggplant, cut into ½-inch-thick slices

3 tablespoons extra-virgin olive oil

4 swordfish steaks

2 tablespoons balsamic vinegar

4 vine-ripened tomatoes

1⅓ cups fresh baby mozzarella cheese

1 handful fresh basil

Make the salsa verde by combining the parsley, pickles, capers, anchovies, and garlic in a bowl, then whisking in the red wine vinegar and olive oil. Set aside.

Brush the eggplant slices with some of the olive oil and cook under a hot broiler until golden brown on both sides. Drain on paper towels.

Cut the swordfish steaks diagonally into three pieces. Heat a little more oil in a large frying pan and cook the swordfish over high heat until golden brown and cooked through. Leave the fish in the pan and add the balsamic vinegar. Cook until sticky.

Cut the tomatoes and mozzarella into thick slices. Layer the eggplant, basil, tomato, mozzarella, and swordfish, and drizzle with the salsa verde dressing.

SERVES 4

seafood

chili crab

2 Dungeness or blue crabs
1/2 cup peanut oil
4 garlic cloves, minced
1 tablespoon grated fresh ginger
2 onions, finely chopped
4 small red chilies, seeded and finely chopped
1/2 cup tomato ketchup
1/2 cup chili sauce
2 tablespoons sugar
1 tablespoon tamarind concentrate
1 tablespoon soy sauce
cilantro leaves, to garnish
steamed rice, to serve

Clean the crabs and remove the hairy dead man's fingers (gills). Use a cleaver to cut each crab into quarters, then crack the claws with the back of the cleaver.

Heat the oil in a wok until hot, or until a cube of bread browns in 15 seconds when added to the oil. Fry the crab pieces in batches until they turn bright orange. Drain off half the oil and discard.

Reheat the remaining oil and cook the garlic, ginger, onions, and chilies over medium heat for 3 minutes. Stir in the sauces and sugar, and bring to a boil.

Return the crab to the wok and cook for 10 minutes. Finally, season with the tamarind concentrate and soy sauce, and garnish with cilantro leaves. Serve immediately with steamed rice.

SERVES 4–6

whole lemongrass fish with sticky chili sauce

1 lemongrass stem, halved and cut into 2-inch lengths
1 large red snapper or sea bass (1¾ lb), incised in three
    places at its thickest part
oil, for deep-frying
5 red Asian shallots, sliced
4 garlic cloves, sliced
2 tablespoons vegetable oil
2 bird's-eye chilies, thinly sliced
½ cup grated jaggery or soft brown sugar
¼ cup fish sauce
¼ cup tamarind concentrate
¼ cup lime juice
cilantro leaves, to garnish

Place the lemongrass pieces into the incisions in the snapper. Heat the deep-frying oil in a wok to 350°F, or until a cube of bread browns in 15 seconds when added to it. Deep-fry the fish until one side is crisp and golden. Turn and cook the other side. Remove and drain on paper towels.

Add the shallots and garlic to the wok and cook until golden. Remove. Do not overcook the shallots or garlic, or they will be bitter.

Heat the 2 tablespoons of vegetable oil in a saucepan, add the chilies, jaggery, fish sauce, tamarind concentrate, and lime juice, and stir until the sugar dissolves. Bring to a boil and cook until the sauce is syrupy. Pour the syrup over the crisp fish and serve immediately, garnished with the cilantro leaves, shallots, and garlic.

SERVES 4

salt and pepper calamari

2¼ lb baby squid, cleaned and tubes halved
1 cup milk
2 tablespoons lemon juice
2 tablespoons sea salt
1½ tablespoons white peppercorns
2 teaspoons sugar
2 cups cornstarch
4 egg whites, lightly beaten
oil, for deep-frying
lime wedges, to serve

Pat the squid tubes dry. Place them on a chopping board with the soft insides facing up, and use a sharp knife to make a fine diamond pattern, taking care not to cut all the way through. Cut the tubes into small rectangles and place them in a bowl. Cover with milk and lemon juice, and refrigerate for 15 minutes.

Place the salt, peppercorns, and sugar in a mortar and pestle or spice grinder and pound or process to a fine powder. Transfer to a bowl and stir in the cornstarch. Dip the squid into the egg whites, then toss to coat in the flour mixture, shaking off any excess.

Heat the oil in a large saucepan or wok to 350°F, or until a cube of bread browns in 15 seconds. Cook the squid in batches until crisp and lightly golden. Serve with lime wedges.

SERVES 4 AS A STARTER

poached fish with jasmine papaya salad

1/4 cup jasmine rice

3 garlic cloves

2 small red chilies, finely chopped

3 tablespoons dried shrimp

2 cups finely shredded green papaya

8 cherry tomatoes, quartered

2 tablespoons lime juice

2 tablespoons fish sauce

1 tablespoon grated light jaggery or light brown sugar

1 1/2 cups coconut milk

1 cup fish stock

4 Kaffir lime leaves, finely shredded

2 lemongrass stems, halved lengthwise

1 tablespoon grated fresh ginger

4 firm whitefish fillets, halved through the center

Follow the package instructions to cook the rice. Place the garlic, chilies, and dried shrimp in a mortar and pestle and pound until combined. Transfer to a nonmetallic bowl and stir in the cooked rice, papaya, and tomatoes.

Put the lime juice, fish sauce, and jaggery in a bowl and whisk to combine. Pour the dressing over the salad and toss to combine.

Put the coconut milk, fish stock, lime leaves, lemongrass, and ginger in a large frying pan and heat until just simmering. Add the fish and cook for 5 minutes, or until tender. Remove the fish and boil the coconut milk until slightly thickened.

Serve two fish fillet halves stacked on top of each other with the sauce spooned over. Accompany with a mound of green papaya salad.

SERVES 4

seafood

moroccan seafood tagine

1 lb firm whitefish fillets
1 lb raw shrimp
2 tablespoons vegetable oil
1 large onion, chopped
1 teaspoon ground ginger
pinch saffron threads
2 teaspoons ground coriander
2 teaspoons ground cumin
1/2 teaspoon chili powder
1 teaspoon ground cinnamon
2 medium orange sweet
    potatoes, peeled and cut
    into chunks

2 medium potatoes, cut into
    chunks
2 tomatoes, chopped
2 zucchini, cut into thick slices
1 cup prunes
1 tablespoon honey
1 tablespoon sliced preserved
    lemon
1 1/2 cups couscous
2 tablespoons butter
1 teaspoon orange-blossom
    water
2 tablespoons slivered almonds,
    toasted

Preheat oven to 350°F. Cut the fish into large cubes. Peel and devein the
shrimp; leave the tails intact. Heat the oil in a large casserole dish, add the
onion and spices, and cook over medium heat for 5 minutes, or until the
onion is soft and the spices are fragrant. Add the vegetables and 2 cups of
water and cook, covered, in the oven for 40 minutes. Remove the lid, add
the seafood, prunes, honey, and preserved lemon, and cook, uncovered, for
another 10 minutes.

Place the couscous in a bowl with the butter and orange-blossom water, and
just cover with boiling water. Allow to stand for 10 minutes, or until all the
liquid has been absorbed. Serve the couscous in a ring with the tagine in the
center. Sprinkle with the almonds.

SERVES 4

NOTE: Preserved lemons are available from delicatessens, specialty food
stores, and Middle Eastern groceries.

summer crab and bean salad

¾ cup dried cannellini beans
1 red bell pepper, cut into large pieces
3 garlic cloves, minced
1 large handful Italian parsley, chopped
½ cup lemon juice
3 tablespoons extra-virgin olive oil
1½ cups fresh or canned crabmeat
1 red onion, thinly sliced
salt and cracked black pepper, to season
crusty bread, to serve

Soak the cannellini beans in cold water overnight.

Drain the beans, place them in a large saucepan, cover with water, and bring to a boil. Reduce the heat and simmer for 20 minutes. Drain and allow the cooked beans to cool slightly.

Cook the bell pepper, skin-side up, under a hot broiler until the skin blackens and blisters. Place in a plastic bag and leave to cool, then peel away the skin, cut into strips, and add to the beans. Stir in the garlic, parsley, lemon juice, olive oil, crabmeat, and red onion, and refrigerate for 2 hours. Season generously with salt and cracked black pepper. Serve with crusty bread.

SERVES 4–6

mediterranean pickled seafood salad

3 tablespoons olive oil
½ cup white wine vinegar
⅔ cup dry white wine
3 garlic cloves, thinly sliced
1 lb black mussels, cleaned and
  debearded
2¼ lb baby octopus, cleaned
2¼ lb squid, cleaned and sliced
1 lb raw shrimp, peeled and
  deveined, tails left intact

shredded zest of 1 lemon
shredded zest of 1 orange
¾ cup sun-dried tomatoes in oil
4 scallions, sliced
1 tablespoon thyme
1 tablespoon basil, shredded
3 tablespoons lemon juice
crusty bread, to serve
lemon wedges, to serve

Place the olive oil, vinegar, white wine, and garlic in a saucepan. Bring to a boil and simmer over low heat for 10 minutes. Add the mussels and cook for 5 minutes, or until the shells open. Remove the mussels from the pan, discarding any that have not opened, and remove the meat from the shells, placing it in a large bowl.

Add the octopus to the pickling liquid and cook for 40 minutes, or until tender. Remove and add the squid and shrimp, and cook for 5 minutes. Drain and discard the liquid.

Add the zests, tomatoes (with their oil), scallions, thyme, basil, and lemon juice to the seafood and mix to combine. Cover and refrigerate for 24–48 hours. Return to room temperature and serve with crusty bread and lemon wedges.

SERVES 4

salmon on skordalia with saffron-lime butter

SKORDALIA
3 medium boiling potatoes,
   peeled and diced
3 garlic cloves, minced
juice of 1 lime
1/3 cup milk
2/3 cup virgin olive oil

SAFFRON-LIME BUTTER
1/3 cup butter
pinch saffron threads
2 tablespoons lime juice

4 salmon fillets, approximately
   1/2 lb each
2 tablespoons oil, for frying
1 tablespoon shredded lime
   zest, to garnish
chervil, to garnish

To make the skordalia, cook the potatoes until soft, then drain and place into a food processor. Process the potatoes, garlic, lime juice, milk, and olive oil until smooth and creamy.

To make the saffron-lime butter, melt the butter in a small saucepan, add the saffron and lime juice, and cook until the butter turns a nutty brown color.

Pat the salmon fillets dry. Heat the oil in a frying pan and cook the salmon, skin-side down, over high heat for 2–3 minutes on each side, or until the skin is crisp and golden brown. Turn and cook the other side.

Serve the salmon on top of the skordalia with the saffron-lime butter spooned over the top. Garnish with lime zest and chervil.

SERVES 4

seafood

teriyaki barbecued salmon

12 dried Chinese mushrooms

1 teaspoon dashi granules

3 tablespoons Japanese soy
  sauce

2 tablespoons mirin

1/2 teaspoon superfine sugar

4 salmon cutlets, 1/3 lb each

3 tablespoons teriyaki marinade

1 tablespoon honey

1 teaspoon sesame oil

9 oz dried soba noodles

1 tablespoon vegetable oil

2 scallions, sliced diagonally

Rehydrate the mushrooms in 2 cups of boiling water. To make the broth, pour the liquid in which the mushrooms were soaked into a saucepan. Add the dashi granules, soy sauce, mirin, and superfine sugar, and bring to a boil. Lower the heat and simmer for 5 minutes.

Place the salmon, mushrooms, teriyaki marinade, honey, and sesame oil into a nonmetallic dish and allow to marinate for 15 minutes.

Bring a large saucepan of water to a boil and cook the noodles for 3–4 minutes, or until tender. Drain.

Heat the oil on a preheated barbecue. Take the salmon and mushrooms out of the marinade and cook over high heat for 3 minutes on each side. (Do not overcook the salmon—it should be slightly rare in the center.) Pour the reserved marinade from the fish over the salmon and mushrooms during cooking.

To serve, divide the noodles between four serving bowls, pour the broth from the mushrooms over the noodles, top with the salmon and mushrooms, and sprinkle with the scallions.

SERVES 4

rainbow trout smoked in grape leaves

1 cup hickory smoking chips
1/2 cup dry white wine
4 medium rainbow trout
1 lemon, thinly sliced
4 oregano sprigs
8 preserved grape leaves

PRESERVED LEMON BUTTER
1/2 cup butter
1 tablespoon chopped oregano
1 tablespoon preserved lemon,
 pith and flesh removed, peel
 finely chopped
1 garlic clove, minced

Preheat a covered barbecue until the charcoal briquettes turn white. Place the smoking chips and wine in a nonmetallic bowl and allow to stand for 15 minutes.

Pat the trout dry using paper towels and place a few slices of lemon and a sprig of oregano into the cavity of each fish. Wrap two grape leaves around each trout and secure with kitchen string. Sprinkle the smoking chips over the hot coals. Place the trout on a lightly oiled barbecue rack, cover, and allow to smoke for 10 minutes or until tender.

To make the preserved lemon butter, mix together the butter, oregano, lemon peel, and garlic. Spread the butter on a lightly greased baking sheet to a 1/2–3/4-inch thickness and freeze until solid. Cut the butter into squares and serve on top of the hot smoked trout.

SERVES 4

NOTE: Preserved lemons are available from delicatessens, specialty food stores, and Middle Eastern groceries.

tuna steaks with wasabi butter

7 oz green tea noodles
1 tablespoon peanut oil
4 tuna steaks
1/3 cup butter, softened
1 tablespooon wasabi paste
2 tablespoons soy sauce
2 teaspoons sesame oil

Cook the noodles in a large saucepan of boiling water until tender. Drain well.

Heat the oil in a large nonstick frying pan and fry the tuna over high heat until cooked to your taste.

To make the wasabi butter, stir together the softened butter and wasabi.

Serve the steaks topped with a nest of noodles and a good spoonful of wasabi butter. Drizzle with the combined soy sauce and sesame oil.

SERVES 4

shrimp, lime, and lemongrass risotto

2¼ lb raw shrimp
6 cups shrimp stock
1 cup dry white wine
2 tablespoons butter
1 tablespoon olive oil
2 garlic cloves, minced
1 small red chili, finely chopped
2 tablespoons finely chopped lemongrass, white part only
4 scallions, chopped
4 Kaffir lime leaves, finely shredded
2 cups risotto rice
1 tablespoon fish sauce
salt and pepper, to season
1 tablespoon Thai basil

Peel and devein the shrimp, leaving the tails intact on some of them (you can use the shrimp shells to make the stock). Chop the shrimp without tails.

Place the stock and white wine in a pan and keep at simmering point.

Heat the butter and oil in a pan, add the garlic, chili, lemongrass, scallions, and Kaffir lime leaves, and cook over medium heat for 3 minutes, or until the lemongrass is fragrant. Add the rice and cook, stirring, for a minute to coat the rice with butter. Add a ladleful of simmering stock, stirring constantly until the stock is almost all absorbed before adding another ladleful. Continue stirring and adding the stock for about 15 minutes, then add the shrimp (chopped and whole). Cook for another 5 minutes, or until all the stock has been added, the rice is tender and creamy, and the shrimp are pink. Stir in the fish sauce, season well with salt and pepper, and serve immediately, sprinkled with the basil.

SERVES 4

seafood

garlic and pepper seafood stir-fry

1 tablespoon Szechuan peppercorns

1 tablespoon sea salt

3 garlic cloves, minced

$^2/_3$ lb calamari tubes, cut into $^1/_2$-inch strips

1 lb raw shrimp, peeled and deveined, tails
   left intact

$^1/_2$ lb scallops, roe removed

2 tablespoons peanut oil

1 tablespoon grated fresh ginger

$^1/_4$ cup sweet chili sauce

Heat a wok until very hot, and dry-fry the Szechuan pepper until fragrant. Transfer to a spice grinder or mortar and pestle with the sea salt, and grind together to crack the peppercorns (don't reduce the mix to a powder). Mix with the garlic and then toss with the seafood to coat.

Heat the oil in the wok until very hot, add the seafood and ginger in batches, and stir-fry over high heat until the shrimp are pink and tender.

Return all the seafood to the wok and add the sweet chili sauce. Cook until the sauce is thick and syrupy, then serve with rice.

SERVES 4

crispy seafood noodle balls

7 oz fresh thick Asian egg nooodles
1/2 lb raw shrimp meat
1/2 lb red drum fillets
3 red Asian shallots, chopped
1 teaspoon ground coriander
1 teaspoon ground cumin
1 teaspoon fish sauce
1 teaspoon sweet chili sauce, plus extra, to serve
2 tablespoons chopped cilantro leaves
oil, for deep-frying
lime juice, to serve

Separate the noodles, pour boiling water over them, and allow to stand for 2 minutes to soften. Rinse under cold water, drain, pat dry, and cut into short lengths.

Place the shrimp meat, fish, shallots, coriander, and cumin in a food processor and process until smooth. Transfer to a bowl and stir in the fish sauce, chili sauce, cilantro, and noodles. Shape the mixture into 12 walnut-size balls, allowing the noodles to hang loosely.

Heat the oil until a cube of bread browns in 10 seconds when added to the wok, or until a little of the mixture floats and sizzles when added to the oil. Deep-fry the balls in batches for 3 minutes, or until golden and cooked through. Serve with sweet chili sauce and a squeeze of lime juice.

MAKES 12

seafood

pork and shrimp spring rolls with bean thread vermicelli

1¾ oz bean thread vermicelli
1 tablespoon peanut oil
2 garlic cloves, minced
1 tablespoon chopped cilantro root
3 red Asian shallots, finely chopped
¼ lb ground pork
¼ lb chopped shrimp meat
2 tablespoons fish sauce
2 tablespoons grated jaggery, or soft brown sugar
1 cup bean sprouts
2 tablespoons chopped cilantro leaves
12 spring roll wrappers
1 egg white, lightly beaten
oil, for deep-frying
sweet chili sauce, to serve

Cover the vermicelli with boiling water for 15 minutes, or until soft. Drain and pat dry. Cut into 2-inch lengths.

Heat the oil in a wok, add the garlic, cilantro root, and shallots, and stir-fry for another 5 minutes. Remove the wok from the heat and transfer the contents into a bowl. Stir in the fish sauce and jaggery, and set aside to cool. Fold in the bean sprouts and cilantro leaves.

Place one heaping tablespoon of the mixture onto one corner of each spring roll wrapper, brush the edges lightly with egg white, and roll up to enclose the filling. Repeat until the filling is used up. Heat the oil in a clean wok until hot. Deep-fry the spring rolls in batches until crisp. Serve with sweet chili sauce.

MAKES 12

rice noodle rolls filled with shrimp

18 oz fresh rice noodle sheets,
   at room temperature
1 teaspoon sesame oil
1 tablespoon peanut oil
1 tablespoon grated fresh ginger
3 scallions, thinly sliced
1¼ cups canned water
   chestnuts, chopped
1 lb raw shrimp, peeled,
   deveined, and chopped

1 tablespoon fish sauce
1 tablespoon soft brown sugar
1 tablespoon snipped garlic
   chives, plus extra, for garnish
2 tablespoons vegetable oil
¼ cup light soy sauce
1 teaspoon sesame oil, extra
½ teaspoon sugar

Open out the rice noodle sheets and cut out eight 6-inch pieces.

Heat the sesame and peanut oils in a wok, add the ginger and scallions, and cook over medium heat for 2 minutes. Add the water chestnuts and shrimp, and cook, stirring, for 5 minutes, or until the shrimp turn pink. Stir in the fish sauce, sugar, and chives. Remove from the pan to cool slightly.

Spoon the mixture down the center of each rice noodle sheet and roll over to enclose the filling.

Heat the vegetable oil in a clean nonstick frying pan. Cook the noodle rolls in batches over medium heat until golden on both sides. Serve drizzled with the combined soy sauce, sesame oil, and sugar, and garnish with extra garlic chives.

MAKES 8

NOTE: Make sure you keep unprepared rice noodle sheets unrefrigerated, or they will split when you unroll them.

seafood

gado gado with chicken

PEANUT SAUCE
1 tablespoon peanut oil
2 garlic cloves, minced
2 small red chilies, finely chopped
3 tablespoons crunchy peanut butter
1/2 cup coconut milk
2 tablespoons kecap manis
2 tablespoons lime juice

10 1/2 oz fresh thin egg noodles
2 boneless, skinless chicken breasts
2 1/2 cups yard-long beans, cut into 2-inch lengths
2 carrots, thinly sliced
1 cucumber, sliced
4 hard-boiled eggs, peeled and quartered
1 cup bean sprouts
fried onion flakes, to garnish

To make the peanut sauce, heat the oil in a saucepan, add the garlic and chilies, and cook until the garlic is soft. Add the remaining ingredients and cook, stirring occasionally, until the sauce thickens.

Cook the noodles in boiling water for 5 minutes, or until tender. Drain.

Place the chicken in a frying pan, cover with water, and bring to a boil. Remove from the heat and let stand for 15 minutes, or until tender. Cool the chicken slightly, then slice thinly.

Steam the beans until tender, drain, and rinse under cold water. Cook the carrots in the same way. Layer the noodles, beans, carrots, cucumber, chicken, eggs, and sprouts on a platter, drizzle with the peanut sauce, and serve garnished with onion flakes.

SERVES 4–6

chicken ravioli with cilantro

1 lb ground chicken

2 tablespoons sweet chili sauce

3 tablespoons chopped cilantro, plus extra leaves for garnishing

1½ teaspoons sesame oil

2 teaspoons grated lime zest

7 oz wonton wrappers

½ cup fish sauce

2 tablespoons soft brown sugar

1 tablespoon peanut oil

1 tablespoon lime juice

1 red chili, thinly sliced

Mix together the chicken, sweet chili sauce, cilantro, sesame oil, and lime zest. Place a heaping tablespoon of the mixture in the center of a wonton wrapper, lightly brush the edges with water, and top with another wrapper. Press the edges together to seal. Repeat with the remaining chicken filling and wrappers.

Cook the ravioli in batches in a large pan of rapidly boiling water for 5 minutes, then drain well and place on serving plates.

Meanwhile, combine the fish sauce, sugar, peanut oil, and lime juice. Pour over the ravioli and garnish with the red chili and extra cilantro leaves.

SERVES 4 AS A FIRST COURSE

poultry

game hens roasted with lemon and garden thyme

4 game hens
2 lemons, quartered
4 garlic cloves, unpeeled
thyme sprigs
3 tablespoons butter, softened
salt and pepper, to season
12 small fingerling potatoes
1 tablespoon oil
1 tablespoon all-purpose flour
$\frac{1}{2}$ cup dry white wine
$1\frac{1}{4}$ cups chicken stock

Preheat the oven to 425°F. Stuff each bird with a lemon quarter, garlic clove, and a few sprigs of thyme. Tie the legs together with string. Spread the hen breasts with butter. Season the skin generously with salt and pepper.

Place the birds on a rack in a baking dish. Toss the potatoes in the oil and sprinkle over the bottom of the dish. Bake for 30 minutes, or until the hen juices run clear when you insert a skewer into the thigh.

Remove the hens and potatoes from the dish and keep warm. Drain off the fat, leaving just the pan juices. Sprinkle with the flour and stir over low heat until smooth. Gradually stir in the wine and stock until the gravy boils and thickens, then simmer for 5 minutes. Serve over the hens and potatoes.

SERVES 4

chicken, okra, and scallion yakitori

¼ cup mirin
¼ cup sake
2 tablespoons sugar
⅓ cup Japanese soy sauce
2¼ lb boneless, skinless chicken thighs
8 large scallions, cut into short lengths
8 small okras, halved

Soak 12 bamboo skewers in water for 15 minutes to prevent scorching. Put the mirin, sake, sugar, and soy sauce in a pan and bring to a boil. Reduce the heat and simmer for 5 minutes, or until slightly thickened.

Cut the chicken into large cubes. Thread the chicken, scallions, and okras onto the skewers.

Grill on a lightly oiled barbecue plate or cook under a broiler until the juices start to flow from the chicken. Baste generously with the sauce and continue to cook, basting often, until the chicken is cooked through. Brush with the remaining sauce and serve.

MAKES 12 SKEWERS

poultry

sesame chicken katsu

4 boneless, skinless chicken breasts
all-purpose flour, for dusting
2 eggs, lightly beaten
$\frac{1}{2}$ cup sesame seeds
2 cups Japanese bread crumbs
oil, for shallow-frying
3 tablespoons tonkatsu sauce
2 tablespoons mirin
3 tablespoons teriyaki sauce

Trim the chicken, place between two sheets of plastic wrap, and flatten to $\frac{3}{4}$ inch thick. Toss the chicken in the flour, shaking off any excess.

Dip the chicken in the egg, then coat in the combined sesame seeds and bread crumbs.

Heat the oil in a large, deep frying pan and cook the chicken in batches over medium heat for 10 minutes, turning once, until the chicken is cooked through. Drain on paper towels.

To make the sauce, put the tonkatsu sauce, mirin, and teriyaki sauce in a pan and heat until the sauce comes to a boil and thickens slightly. Serve with the chicken and a bowl of steamed Japanese rice.

SERVES 4

quick peking duck

1 Chinese roasted duck, chopped
1 package Mandarin pancakes
3 tablespoons hoisin sauce
1 tablespoon plum sauce
1 cucumber, cut into long lengths
6 scallions, cut into long lengths

Remove the bones from the duck if it has not been done, and cut the skin and flesh into small squares.

Put the pancakes in a large bamboo steamer over a wok of simmering water, making sure the base of the steamer isn't sitting in the water. Steam for 3 minutes, or until warm. (You can also heat the pancakes in the microwave.)

Mix together the hoisin and plum sauces.

Serve each pancake with a little duck, cucumber, and scallion, with the sauce drizzled over. Fold the pancakes to enclose the filling.

SERVES 4–6 AS A LIGHT DINNER OR STARTER

NOTE: You can buy roasted ducks in most Asian grocery stores. Ask for the duck to be chopped and, if possible, boned.

satay chicken and mushroom pies

2–4 sheets puff pastry
1 tablespoon peanut oil
4 scallions, sliced
⅓ lb oyster mushrooms
⅓ lb enoki mushrooms
6 boneless, skinless chicken thighs, cut into small cubes
3 tablespoons satay sauce
1 cup coconut milk
2 tablespoons chopped cilantro
1 egg, lightly beaten

Preheat the oven to 400°F. Cut rounds from the pastry to fit the tops of four 1½-cup ovenproof dishes.

Heat the oil in a large frying pan and cook the scallions and mushrooms over medium heat until soft.

Add the chicken and cook until browned. Stir in the satay sauce and cook until fragrant.

Add the coconut milk and cilantro and bring to a boil. Reduce the heat and simmer for 10 minutes, or until the sauce thickens slightly.

Spoon the filling into the dishes (leave a bit of space at the top). Cover with the pastry tops, then brush with beaten egg. Cut a steam hole in the center of each pie and bake for 20 minutes, or until the pastry is crisp and golden.

SERVES 4

lamb cutlets with creamy spinach

8 French lamb chops
freshly cracked black pepper, to coat
1 tablespoon olive oil
2 tablespoons butter
2 garlic cloves, minced
4 scallions, sliced
9 cups baby spinach leaves, roughly chopped
1 tablespoon shredded basil
3 tablespoons light whipping cream
2 tablespoons whole-grain mustard
4 tomatoes, halved and roasted

Trim the lamb chops of any excess fat or sinew and lightly coat each chop in a little cracked black pepper.

Heat the oil in a frying pan and cook the chops in batches over high heat for 3 minutes on each side, or until cooked to your liking. Remove from the pan and keep warm.

Melt the butter in the frying pan and add the garlic, scallions, and spinach. Cook until the scallions are soft and the spinach wilts, then add the basil, cream, and mustard, and cook until heated through.

Serve the creamy spinach topped with the peppered lamb chops and warm roasted tomatoes.

SERVES 4

rice-stick noodles with kecap beef

8 oz narrow, dried rice-stick noodles
3 tablespoons peanut oil
2/3 lb sirloin steak, sliced
2 garlic cloves, minced
1 lemongrass stem, white part only, finely chopped
3 scallions, sliced into 1¼-inch lengths
2 cups snap peas
1 bunch broccolini or baby broccoli, roughly chopped
3 tablespoons kecap manis
2 tablespoons soy sauce
1 tablespoon fish sauce
2 tablespoons snipped garlic chives

Pour boiling water over the noodles and allow them to stand for 10 minutes, or until tender. Drain.

Heat half the oil in a wok, add the meat, garlic, and lemongrass in batches, and stir-fry over high heat until the meat is browned. Add the scallions and the green vegetables, and stir-fry until bright green and tender but still slightly crisp. Remove and keep warm.

Add the remaining oil to the wok and then the noodles. Stir-fry for 1 minute. Stir in the kecap manis, soy sauce, and fish sauce to coat the noodles.

Return the meat and the vegetables to the wok, along with any juices, and heat through. Stir the chives through the dish and serve immediately.

SERVES 4

veal with capers and white wine

4 veal cutlets
all-purpose flour, for dusting
2 tablespoons oil
1 tablespoon butter
2 small leeks, white part only, sliced
1 cup dry white wine
$1/2$ cup capers
1 cup chicken stock
2 tablespoons lemon juice
3 tablespoons butter, chopped

Pound the veal cutlets flat. Toss in the flour and shake off any excess.

Heat the oil and butter in a large nonstick frying pan and cook the veal in batches until crisp and golden on both sides. Drain on paper towels and keep warm.

Add the leeks to the pan and cook for 5 minutes, or until golden. Add the wine and capers and bring to a boil. Boil until almost all evaporated.

Add the stock and boil until reduced by half. Reduce the heat and stir in the lemon juice and chopped butter. Return the veal to the pan and cook for 3 minutes to heat through. Best served with mashed potatoes.

SERVES 4

cabernet beef with lentils

4 pieces rib-eye beef tenderloin
1 cup cabernet sauvignon
1 tablespoon red wine vinegar
2 tablespoons red currant jelly
1 tablespoon Dijon mustard
4 garlic cloves, sliced
4 oregano sprigs
1½ cups French green lentils
2 tablespoons butter
2 tablespoons oil
grated zest of 1 orange
4 shallots, finely chopped

Trim the beef and put into a shallow nonmetallic dish. Mix the wine, vinegar, jelly, mustard, garlic, and oregano, and pour over the beef. Leave for 10 minutes.

Put the lentils in a saucepan with 2½ cups water. Bring to a boil, then reduce the heat and simmer for 20 minutes, or until the lentils are tender. Drain.

Heat the butter and half the oil in a frying pan, add the orange zest and shallots, and cook over medium heat until golden. Add the lentils and cook for 5 minutes to heat through. Remove and keep warm.

Drain the beef, reserving the marinade. Heat the remaining oil and fry the steaks over high heat until cooked to your taste. Remove the steaks and add the marinade to the pan. Bring to a boil and cook until thickened slightly. Serve the lentils and steak drizzled with sauce.

SERVES 4

rosemary filet mignon with blue cheese spread

8 slices pancetta
4 long rosemary sprigs
4 beef filet mignon (tenderloin) steaks
$1/3$ cup soft cream cheese
$2/3$ cup creamy blue cheese
1 tablespoon oil

Wrap two folded slices of pancetta and a sprig of rosemary around the outside of each steak, securing with kitchen string.

Beat together the cream cheese and blue cheese.

Heat the oil in a frying pan or broiling pan and fry or broil the steak using medium heat until cooked to your taste. Top with the cheese spread and serve with a few new potatoes.

SERVES 4

garlic creamed beans with herby lamb

4 lamb racks, each with
   3 chops (ask your butcher
   to trim them)
1 tablespoon oil
salt and pepper, to season
2 garlic cloves, sliced
2 bay leaves, torn
4 tablespoons mint-flavored
   apple jelly
1 tablespoon red wine vinegar

GARLIC CREAMED BEANS
2 cups canned cannellini
   or lima beans
2 cups chicken stock
1 bay leaf
2 garlic cloves, minced
1 tablespoon extra-virgin
   olive oil
2 tablespoons butter
salt and pepper, to season

Preheat the oven to 425°F. Put the lamb in a baking dish, brush lightly with the oil, and season well with salt and pepper. Cut small slits in the top of the lamb and insert slices of garlic and bits of bay leaf.

Combine the mint-flavored jelly and vinegar, and brush some over the lamb, keeping the rest for the sauce. Bake for 20 minutes, or until cooked to your taste. Remove from the baking dish and leave to stand for 5 minutes before slicing.

To make the beans, put the beans, stock, and bay leaf in a pan and bring to a boil. Reduce the heat and simmer for 10 minutes. Drain ⅔ cup of the stock from the beans and set aside for the sauce. Remove the bay leaf. Transfer to a food processor, add the garlic, oil, and butter, and process until creamy. Season with salt and pepper, cover, and keep warm.

Transfer the baking dish to the stovetop, add the reserved stock and mint-flavored jelly, and bring to a boil. Boil until syrupy.

Serve the creamed beans and lamb with the sauce poured over the top.

SERVES 4

chili beef with cheese quesadillas

1 tablespoon oil
2 garlic cloves, minced
2 onions, sliced
3 small red chilies, finely
  chopped
1 large red bell pepper, sliced
1 lb lean ground beef
1½ cups canned red kidney
  beans, rinsed and drained
¾ cup bottled tomato salsa
2 teaspoons sugar

QUESADILLAS
8 flour tortillas
2 tablespoons oil
1 cup firmly packed grated
  cheddar cheese
3 scallions, sliced
2 tablespoons sliced green
  jalapeño peppers

Heat the oil in a large frying pan, add the garlic, onions, chilies, and bell pepper, and cook over medium heat for 5 minutes, or until the onion is golden.

Add the beef and brown over high heat. Drain off any excess liquid. Add the beans, salsa, and sugar, and cook over medium heat for 10 minutes, or until thick.

To make the quesadillas, brush one side of each tortilla with oil. Heat a large nonstick frying pan and place a tortilla, oiled-side down, in the pan. Sprinkle with some cheese, scallions, and jalapeños, and then top with another tortilla, oiled-side up. Fry over medium heat until the base is crisp and golden. Turn and cook until the tortilla is golden brown and the cheese has melted. Keep warm while you cook the rest.

Serve bowls of chili beef with the cheese quesadillas on the side.

SERVES 4

meat

tandoori lamb chops with melon raita

12 lamb loin chops
1 tablespoon lemon juice
3 tablespoons tandoori paste
¾ cup plain yogurt

MELON RAITA
½ lb honeydew melon, peeled and diced
½ red onion, diced
1 garlic clove, minced
1 tablespoon finely shredded mint
3 tablespoons shredded coconut
2 teaspoons lemon juice

Put the lamb chops in a shallow nonmetallic dish. Drizzle with the lemon juice. Combine the tandoori paste and yogurt, pour over the lamb, and toss well. Cover and leave for 10 minutes.

To make the raita, combine all the ingredients in a bowl.

Broil or barbecue the lamb chops on high heat for 3 minutes each side or until cooked to your taste. Serve with the melon raita.

SERVES 4

pork with sweet cider apples

1²/₃ lb pork tenderloin
36 small sage leaves
12 thin slices prosciutto
1 tablespoon oil
3½ tablespoons butter
2 green apples, cored and sliced
2 small fennel bulbs, sliced
1 cup hard apple cider
1 cinnamon stick
1 tablespoon white wine vinegar
1 teaspoon soft brown sugar

Preheat the oven to 350°F. Trim the pork of fat.

Press the sage leaves onto the outside of the tenderloin. Wrap the prosciutto around the pork in a spiral pattern so that the sage leaves are visible. Secure with skewers.

Heat the oil in a nonstick frying pan and brown the pork over high heat.

Transfer to a baking dish and cook in the oven for 15 minutes, or until tender. Leave to stand for 5 minutes before cutting into thick slices.

Melt the butter in a frying pan and fry the apples and fennel over medium heat for 10 minutes, or until golden brown. Increase the heat, add the cider and cinnamon, and cook, stirring to scrape up any bits on the bottom of the pan. Add the white wine vinegar and brown sugar, bring to a boil, and cook until the sauce has reduced by half. Remove the cinnamon. Serve the apple and fennel slices with the sliced pork on top. Drizzle with the pan juices.

SERVES 4

meat

sweet ginger and chili vegetables with rice noodles

18 oz fresh rice noodle sheets, at room temperature

2 tablespoons oil

1 teaspoon sesame oil

3 tablespoons grated fresh ginger

1 onion, thinly sliced

1 red bell pepper, sliced

¼ lb fresh shiitake mushrooms, sliced

1¼ cups baby corn

1 lb Chinese kale, sliced

2 cups snow peas

3 tablespoons sweet chili sauce

2 tablespoons fish sauce

2 tablespoons dark soy sauce

1 tablespoon lime juice

16 Thai basil leaves

Cut the noodle sheets into 1¼-inch-wide strips, then cut each strip into three. Gently separate the noodles (you may need to run a little cold water over them to do this).

Heat the oils in a wok, add the ginger and onion, and stir-fry until the onion is soft. Add the remaining vegetables and stir-fry until brightly colored and just tender.

Add the noodles to the vegetables and stir-fry until the noodles start to soften. Stir in the combined sauces and lime juice, and cook until heated through. Remove from the heat and toss the basil leaves through the dish.

SERVES 4

spiced honey eggplant and sweet potato

3 tablespoons olive oil

12 slender eggplants, trimmed
and halved

1 medium orange sweet potato,
peeled and cut into chunks

3 garlic cloves, minced

2 tablespoons grated fresh
ginger

4 scallions, sliced

2 teaspoons ground cumin

1/2 teaspoon cayenne pepper

3 tablespoons honey

2 tablespoons lemon juice

COUSCOUS

1¼ cups couscous

1 cinnamon stick

2 tablespoons butter

pinch saffron threads

2 cups boiling vegetable stock
or water

2/3 cup cashews

plain yogurt and harissa,
to serve

Heat half the oil in a large frying pan and cook the eggplant and sweet potato in batches until browned on both sides. Remove from the pan.

Add the rest of the oil to the pan and cook the garlic, ginger, and scallions until soft. Add the spices and cook until fragrant. Return the eggplant and scallions to the pan, add the combined honey, lemon juice, and 1¼ cups of water, and simmer for 15–20 minutes, or until tender, stirring the vegetables occasionally so they cook evenly.

To make the couscous, put the couscous, cinnamon, butter, and saffron in a bowl. Add the boiling stock or water and leave until all the liquid is absorbed. Fluff with a fork to separate the grains and remove the cinnamon stick.

Serve the couscous topped with the eggplant and sweet potato. Sprinkle with cashews and finish with a dollop of plain yogurt and a little harissa.

SERVES 4

vegetables

artichoke risoni

2 tablespoons butter
1 tablespoon olive oil
2 fennel bulbs, sliced
1½ cups marinated artichoke hearts, drained and chopped
1¼ cups light whipping cream
1 tablespoon Dijon mustard
3 tablespoons dry white wine
½ cup grated Parmesan cheese
1⅔ cups risoni
2 cups shredded spinach

Heat the butter and olive oil in a frying pan and cook the fennel over medium heat for 20 minutes, or until caramelized. Add the artichokes and cook for 5–10 minutes longer. Add the cream, mustard, wine, and Parmesan, and bring to a boil. Reduce the heat and simmer for 5 minutes.

Meanwhile, cook the pasta in a large saucepan of rapidly boiling water until al dente, then drain. Add the risoni and spinach to the sauce and cook until the spinach has wilted. Excellent served on toasted Italian bread.

SERVES 4

chocolate and frangelico mousse

9 oz semisweet chocolate
1 tablespoon light corn syrup
3 egg whites
2 egg yolks
3 tablespoons Frangelico
⅓ cup light whipping cream

Put the chocolate in a heatproof bowl over a pan of simmering water, making sure the base of the bowl is not sitting in the water. Leave until the chocolate has melted. Remove and allow to cool slightly, then stir in the corn syrup.

Beat the egg whites in a clean dry bowl until stiff peaks form. Stir the egg yolks and Frangelico into the cooled chocolate.

Beat the cream until soft peaks form. Gently fold the cream and egg whites into the chocolate with a large metal spoon or spatula.

Pour the chocolate mousse into serving bowls or cups and refrigerate until firm.

SERVES 4

peach and plum crumbles

1 lb ripe blood plums, halved
1 lb ripe peaches, halved
1/2 cup soft brown sugar
3/4 cup all-purpose flour
8 amaretti cookies, crushed
1/4 cup plus 1 tablespoon butter, chilled and chopped
3 tablespoons sugar

Preheat the oven to 400°F. Put the plum and peach halves on a broiling tray and broil until soft.

Cut the fruit into wedges and arrange in ramekins or a large ovenproof dish. Sprinkle lightly with the brown sugar and toss to coat the fruit.

Mix together the flour and amaretti cookies in a bowl. Add the butter and rub in with your fingertips until the mixture resembles fine bread crumbs. Stir in the sugar and add 2 tablespoons of chilled water. Mix with a flat-bladed knife until the mixture clumps in beads.

Top the fruit with the crumble and bake for 30 minutes, or until the juices from the fruit are oozing through the crumble.

SERVES 4

passion fruit custard pots

1 cup superfine sugar
4 eggs
1 cup light whipping cream
¾ cup plus 2 tablespoons passion fruit pulp
2 tablespoons lime juice
½ cup sugar

Preheat the oven to 315°F. Put the superfine sugar, eggs, cream, passion fruit pulp, and lime juice in a bowl and whisk together.

Pour the mixture into four 1-cup ramekins and place the ramekins in a baking dish. Pour boiling water into the baking dish to come halfway up the sides of the ramekins. Cook for 25 minutes, or until the custards are set. Remove from the dish and allow to cool. Refrigerate for 4 hours before serving.

Put the sugar in a pan over low heat until melted and starting to turn into liquid. Bring slowly to a boil, then boil until it turns a deep caramel color. Pour over the custard pots to cover the surface. Leave to cool and set (don't refrigerate).

SERVES 4

irish coffee semifreddo with praline shards

4 egg yolks
3 tablespoons whiskey
1 tablespoon finely ground
  coffee
1 cup superfine sugar
2 egg whites
2 cups whipped cream

PRALINE
1 cup shelled pistachio nuts
1 tablespoon mint leaves
1 cup sugar
1 tablespoon fresh lavender
  flowers

Put the egg yolks, whiskey, coffee, and half the sugar in a heatproof bowl and beat over a pan of simmering water until the mixture is thick and pale. Remove from the heat to cool.

Whisk the egg whites in a clean dry bowl until soft peaks form. Gradually beat in the remaining sugar until the mixture is thick and glossy.

Fold the egg whites and cream into the cooled mixture and pour into a 9-inch loaf pan. Cover with plastic wrap and freeze until firm.

To make the praline, put the nuts and mint leaves on a large sheet lined with parchment paper. Put the sugar and 3 tablespoons of water in a pan and stir over low heat until the sugar dissolves. Bring to a boil and boil until it turns deep golden brown. Pour over the nuts and mint, then press on some lavender flowers. Leave to cool, then break into large shards.

Serve slices of the semifreddo with shards of praline.

SERVES 4–6

macadamia syrup dumplings

1 cup self-rising flour
1/2 teaspoon ground cinnamon
3 tablespoons butter, chilled and chopped
2/3 cup macadamia nuts, toasted and roughly chopped
1 egg, lightly beaten
1 tablespoon milk
heavy cream, to serve

SYRUP
1 cup raw sugar
3 tablespoons butter
3 tablespoons dark corn or maple syrup
2 tablespoons dark rum
2 tablespoons lemon juice

Sift the flour and cinnamon into a bowl. Add the butter and rub in with your fingertips until the mixture resembles fine bread crumbs. Stir in the nuts. Add the combined egg and milk, and mix to form a soft dough.

To make the syrup, put the sugar, butter, syrup, rum, lemon juice, and 2 cups of water in a saucepan and stir over low heat until the sugar dissolves.

Drop large spoonfuls of the dough into the simmering liquid and cook, covered, for 10 minutes, or until a skewer comes out clean when inserted into the center of a dumpling. Serve with heavy cream.

SERVES 4

chocolate cake with drunken muscatels

1 cup muscat grapes
1½ cups muscatel wine
1 cup superfine sugar
1¾ cups self-rising flour
1 cup baking cocoa
1 teaspoon baking soda
3 tablespoons vegetable oil
2 eggs, lightly beaten
¾ cup buttermilk
thick cream, to serve

CHOCOLATE SAUCE
9 oz semisweet chocolate,
  chopped
1 cup light whipping cream

Put the muscat grapes and muscatel in a saucepan and bring to a boil. Remove from the heat and leave for 4 hours.

Preheat the oven to 350°F. Grease and line a deep 8-inch round cake pan.

Put the sugar, flour, cocoa, baking soda, oil, eggs, and buttermilk in a bowl and beat until smooth.

Spoon into the pan and bake for 40 minutes, or until a skewer comes out clean when inserted into the center. Cool in the pan for 10 minutes before turning out onto a wire rack.

To make the sauce, put the chocolate and cream in a pan and heat gently, stirring, until melted and combined. Drizzle over the cake and serve with the drunken muscatels and thick cream.

SERVES 6–8

index

Published in 2007 by Murdoch Books Pty Limited
www.murdochbooks.com.au

Murdoch Books Australia
Pier 8/9
23 Hickson Road
Millers Point NSW 2000
Phone: +61 (0) 2 8220 2000
Fax: +61 (0) 2 8220 2558

Murdoch Books UK Limited
Erico House
6th Floor
93–99 Upper Richmond Road
Putney, London SW15 2TG
Phone: +44 (0) 20 8785 5995
Fax: +44 (0) 20 8785 5985

Chief Executive: Juliet Rogers
Publishing Director: Kay Scarlett

Design manager: Vivien Valk
Project manager: Janine Flew
Editor: Zoë Harpham
Design concept: Alex Frampton
Designer: Susanne Geppert
Introduction: Leanne Kitchen
Photography: Chris Chen, Ben Dearnley
Styling: Kristen Anderson, Michelle Noerianto, Suzie Smith
Front cover photograph: Ben Dearnley
Food preparation: Michaela Le Compte, Valli Little
Production: Maiya Levitch

Text, design and photography copyright Murdoch Books 2007. All rights reserved.
No part of this publication may be reproduced, stored in a retrieval system or transmitted in any
form or by any means, electronic, mechanical, photocopying, recording or otherwise, without
the prior written permission of the publisher.

ISBN 978-1-74196-002-0

Printed by Midas Printing (Asia) Ltd in 2007. PRINTED IN CHINA.

IMPORTANT: Those who might be at risk from the effects of salmonella poisoning (the elderly,
pregnant women, young children and those suffering from immune deficiency diseases) should
consult their doctor with any concerns about eating raw eggs.

CONVERSION GUIDE: You may find cooking times vary depending on the oven you are using.
For fan-forced ovens, as a general rule, set the oven temperature to 20°C (35°F) lower than
indicated in the recipe. We have used 20 ml (4 teaspoon) tablespoon measures. If you are using
a 15 ml (3 teaspoon) tablespoon, for most recipes the difference will not be noticeable. However,
for recipes using baking powder, gelatine, bicarbonate of soda (baking soda), small amounts of
flour and cornflour (cornstarch), add an extra teaspoon for each tablespoon specified.